I Missed You Quietly Today

I MISSED YOU QUIETLY TODAY

BECKY HEMSLEY

POETRY COPYRIGHT © 2025
BECKY HEMSLEY

All rights reserved.

No part of this publication may be reproduced, stored or transmitted in any form by any means, electronic, mechanical, photocopying or otherwise without the prior written permission of the author.

Becky Hemsley at Wildmark Publishing

EMAIL ENQUIRIES: info@beckyhemsley.com

ISBN HARDCOVER 978-1-915834-23-2
ISBN PAPERBACK 978-1-915834-22-5

For those we've loved and lost.

And for Nick.
I wish I'd had the chance to meet you.

"Give sorrow words; the grief that does not speak knits up the o-er wrought heart and bids it break."

William Shakespeare, Macbeth.

This quote may have been written over 400 years ago, but it is as true today as the day it was penned: grief, and the sorrow that it brings, yearn to be heard. If they are not, they slowly break the heart from the inside out and we continue to grieve lonely and alone.

The difficulty though, lies in not being able to find the words; in not being able to voice the pain in a way that both describes its extremity and provides some reprieve from it. Because how do you put into words such loss? And how do you find peace amongst it?

Well, that's what I set out to do in this book: to try and give grief the gravity it deserves, whilst also offering hope. Peace. Reprieve.
I want you to know that you are not alone; and that even if your heart is breaking, there are others who understand what you're going through.

You don't have to give your sorrow poetic words in order to set it free. Having conversations, writing letters, sharing memories, playing music; they all play their part in allowing you to breathe a little more easily through your loss.

So, if you do anything today, give words to your grief. It might be a chat with a friend. It might be listening to a song that resonates with how you're feeling. And it might be writing a letter to your lost loved one, even though you know you'll never send it.
But your heart will feel it. A weight will lift - even if just for a moment – and it might just give you the space to find that reprieve. That peace. That hope.

"Tu n'es plus là où tu étais mais tu es partout là où je suis."

You are no longer where you were, but you are everywhere I am.

Victor Hugo

CONTENTS

Quietly	11
Holding On	13
When You Meet Again	15
Pennies From Heaven	17
I Wish I Could Say	19
Black Sand	21
Where I'll Be	23
Remembering	25
What I Mean	27
Will It?	29
A Single Moment	31
Somewhere To Go	33
The Thing About The Heart	35
On Hold	37
Holding Space	39
The Ghost Of Love	41
Rocks	43
Guide	45
Shapeshifting	47
Let The Grief Gather	49
Echoes	51
This Too Shall Not Pass	53
Taking Turns	55
Let Them Live	57
Rock, Paper, Scissors	59
Time Waits For No-one	61
One	63
I Still Say It	65
Tightrope	67
Still Standing	69
Stop Start	71
Skies Down	73
Enough	75
Missing A Beat	77
How Do I Grieve Thee?	79
Light Leaks Through	81
How Long Is A Piece Of String	83
Precious Light	85
A Part	87
The Griefcase	89
Searching	91
Be Gentle	93
Grief Is Not A Shoe Size	95
Everyone's Grief	97
The Right Words	99
Take My Sadness	101
Write To Me	103
Nowhere To Go	105
Less	107
Stubborn Love	109
Love Language	111
On The Fence	113
Grief Is A Thief	115
A Candle	117
Back To Life	119
The Guilt I Felt	121
When You Visit	123
Daffodils	125
Pitter Patter	127
I Hope You Find Hope	129
Signs	131

You were like a snowflake:
So entirely unique that there will never be another you.

And yet, I will still scour every snowstorm
in the hopes that I might find you
again.

Quietly

I missed you quietly today. So quietly that no one noticed.

I missed you as I climbed out of bed and as I brushed my teeth; when I waited at the lights on the drive into work and as I heard the rain outside my window.

I missed you as I ordered lunch and as I kicked off my shoes when I got home; as I switched off the lights and climbed into bed for the night.

I missed you without tears or noise or fanfare.
But oh how I felt it.

I felt it in the morning, at lunchtime, in the evening and at night. I felt it as I woke, as I waited, as I worked. I felt it at home, on the road, in the light, in the dark, in the rain.

I felt it in every one of those moments, each one sitting heavier and heavier as the weight of me missing you kept growing and growing.

Yes, I missed you quietly today.

But I felt it so loudly.

What's the heaviest thing you've ever had to hold?

Grief.

Holding On

Loss is an inevitable part of life. And with it of course, comes grief.

Grief can feel like a deep, dark hole that we will never climb out of, but when it all feels hopeless, I like to remember that it works just like love.

Because, when we first fall in love, it is intense.
It is overwhelming and consuming and loud. We cannot think of anything else, and we constantly crave the one we love.

After a while it becomes less intense, but it grows.
It grows deeper, more comfortable. It settles down and settles in for the long haul, knowing that it is not fleeting or superficial. It is less consuming. Quieter. An undercurrent of our every day without overwhelming our every thought.

Sometimes something will happen to bring that overwhelming love back to the surface; moments of pride or surprise or nostalgia that remind us just how much we love someone. Moments where our love is once again intense and loud.
And then it settles back into our heart where it knows it will stay.

Grief is the same.
At first it is loud and consuming, intense and overwhelming.
We constantly crave the one we grieve.

Then it becomes less intense, less consuming. An undercurrent of our every day without overwhelming our every thought. And sometimes something will happen to bring our grief bubbling right back to the surface. Moments where our grief is once again intense and loud.
And then it settles back into our heart where it knows it will stay.

Because great grief is born of great love.

So where grief remains, where grief rests,
it often helps to remember that love is there too.

Sitting with her arm around grief
and holding it tight.

*The emptiness in my arms
is nothing compared to my heart*

When You Meet Again

There are going to be times in life when death steals the people that you love from you. When grief swoops in and descends hungrily and heavily and leaves you feeling empty.

And at those times, it can be hard to get out of bed and open the curtains; to let the light in.

It can be hard to leave the house and speak to people; to let the world in.

It can be hard to know how to go on living when the person you love could not. Hard to see the point in moving forward without them by your side.

But there is one certainty in life.
And that is death.

And one day it will steal you too.

And when that time comes,
wouldn't it be wonderful to be able to regale your loved ones with tales of the adventures you were able to keep having?

Wouldn't it be wonderful to tell them how you took them with you in your heart, and how you felt them by your side every step of the way?

Yes.

Wouldn't it be wonderful to live a life that is so full,
that you simply cannot wait to tell them about it
when you meet again?

*If grief is the price we pay for love,
and love itself is priceless...*

Then how can we ever repay that debt?

Pennies From Heaven

People say that when you
'Find a penny, pick it up'
And all day long, the saying goes,
You'll have the best of luck

But what if all the pennies
That you notice and you find
Aren't coins that have been dropped
Or that somebody left behind?

What if they were never coins
Intended to be spent
But someone reaching out to you
With pennies heaven-sent?

'Cause maybe all those pennies
Are a copper-coloured love
Raining down towards the ground
From silver clouds above

So go out and collect them,
Fill your pockets with their weight
Collect them from the sunrise
And until it's getting late

Then you can store the pennies
All together in a jar
The price of love collecting there
Like monetary stars

And as you let them gather then,
They might remind you how
That copper-coloured cost of love
Is always with you now

But so is love itself because
Coins always have two sides
We pay for love with grief
But that's because the love survives

So, when you see a penny,
Lying, glinting on the floor
And something tells you this is not
Like coins you've found before

Then trust the heart that tells you
'Find a penny, pick it up'
And know that in your pocket
All day long you'll carry love

Try not to fight with your grief my love.
It doesn't want to be here either.

I Wish I Could Say

I wish I could say so much more to you than
"I'm sorry for your loss."

I wish I could say
"let's go and visit them" or
"let's give them a call."

I wish I could tell you that
"you'll see them tomorrow" or
"they're just on their way."

I wish I could ask you to
"send them my love" or to
"pass on my best wishes".

But you can't call them or pass on my best or see them tomorrow.

So instead, I call you
and I listen to you
and I send you flowers.

I say their name as you share your memories; I hold your hand
and I catch your tears.

And I load my words with love and my arms with compassion.
And instead of everything I really wish I could say,
I tell you

"I'm so sorry for your loss."

*Your sand fell through your hourglass
too quickly*

*And now mine won't fall
fast enough*

Black Sand

Living with grief is like pouring buckets of black sand onto a golden beach.

At first, the black is overwhelming. It smothers and eclipses the golden grains of sand, and it absorbs heat quickly, so it burns more readily when you touch it. It hurts too much to pick it up and it pains you to walk over it.

And you know that, to get to the beach underneath, you're going to have to disturb the black sand; to mix it in amongst the gold.
And you don't want to do that. Because then the black will become part of the beach itself.

But after a while, you will start walking again, and the steps you take across the beach will begin to mix the sand together.
Huge chunks of black sand amongst the gold at first.
Huge expanses of black that burn you and hurt you.

But one day, you will look at your beach and realise that you cannot find those huge expanses of black anymore.

And when you look closely at the sand, you will see why:

There will be grains of black nestled amongst every single part of your beach. It will no longer be golden and no longer be black, but something uniquely new; a fusion of the two.

Yes, your beach will go on and the sand will remain.
But it will be forever altered in a way you'll never undo.

You will never extract those grains of grief from your life, and it's futile to try. Because after a day on the beach, it is perfectly normal to find sand everywhere.

On every part of your body and in every part of your home.

And, when the sand is grief...

You'll find it
in every piece of your soul.

But if I listen closely,

*I'll hear the wind whisper your name
and the birds sing your song…*

And I'll know the world remembers you.

Where I'll Be

When I'm no longer with you
And you're looking out for me
I'll be waving from along that line
Where blue sky kisses sea

I'll be resting on the cloud
That's shaped just like a bird that sings
And dancing through the puddles
That have fallen from its wings

I'll be knitting leaves for autumn
With pink blossom in my hair
Whilst sitting on a branch
That lifts me ten feet in the air

I'll be painting all the colours
When the sun begins to rise
And as it comes to set against
The dusky, evening skies

I'll be keeping a collection
Of a hundred billion lights
That I'll be stringing up above the clouds
As stars each night

So when you want to look for me
But don't know where I'm found
Just search the skies, the ocean
And the world that's all around

And look for how I've painted
All the colours of the sun
Look for how the stars all gather
When the day is done

Watch the clouds arrange and change
Themselves through different shapes
Feel the early morning,
Dawning sun upon your face

Watch the blossom from my hair
Appearing on the trees
Watch the rain fall softly
Like my knitted autumn leaves

Then dance through all the puddles,
Climb a branch that's ten-feet high
And wave to me along that line
Where blue sea kisses sky

*I know you're just one star
in an entire sky of them...*

*But you're the only one
I see*

Remembering

Sometimes I get scared that there'll come a day when I don't think about you: a day when you don't cross my mind or enter my head.

And what if that day turns into two days or three days or a week or a month or a year?

What if I forget to remember you?

And when that happens – when I get scared - I sit for a moment and take deep breaths.
In.
Out.
In.
Out.
And that's when I realise…

I am breathing.

And it's not something I have to remember to do.
It's not a conscious thing; most of the time, I don't even recognise it.
I just do it.

Constantly. All the time.
And that's what keeps me going.

And I realise then that remembering you is the same.
It's not something I have to remember to do: I just do it.

We can't forget to remember,
any more than we can remember to forget.

So, you are in my thoughts.
In my mind,
in my head and in my heart.

Constantly. All the time.
And that's what keeps me going.

Because remembering you
is as natural
as breathing.

Don't dis*miss* the way I'm sing*ing you*r name,
as me no longer hurting.

I'm still *missing you.*

What I Mean

When I say *I miss you*, what I really mean
is that...

That little tune you always used to hum, used to whistle, used to sing, is now missing from the soundtrack of my days.

Your hand is now missing from mine whenever I cross the road, and your arms are now missing each time I yearn to be pulled into one of your comforting hugs.

Instead of *I miss you*, what I could say
is that...

You'll never again cook me that meal you always loved to cook, and I'll never again get to taste it, exactly the way you made it.

You'll never again ask me questions about the book I'm reading or the film we watched or how my day has been; and you'll never again send me photos or messages or voice notes of things that remind you of me.

When I say *I miss you*, what I really want to say
is that...

I won't hear the sound of your laughter mixing with mine again, when we share a joke or a story that only we understand, and I won't hear your voice answering me when we reminisce about the past or plan the future.

And it hurts.

You are missing from everything I do and from everything I see.

So when I say *I miss you*, what I really mean...

is that you are missing

from me.

There is a fire in the unscrambling of grief.

So, even when it feels cold,
just know that the flame of love still burns here.

Will It?

Will it get better?
Will it be lighter?
Will it get easier,
Softer and brighter?

Will it grow quiet;
A whisper instead
Of all of the silence
That screams in your head?

Will it be gentle?
Will there come a time
When grief doesn't feel
Like a mountainous climb?

Will it retire,
Or will it remain
As a constant reminder
Of loss and of pain?

Will it grow wings?
Will it ever take flight?
Or will it take rest
In your nest every night?

Will it take everything
You've left to give
By choosing your heart
As the place it will live?

Well, it will be different
It will be changed
Not easy as such
But a life rearranged

A life you'll adjust to
A life built upon
The love that keeps giving
And keeps living on

For grief's reaching out
Trying to settle in place
Trying to join
Not remove or replace

So when it won't quit,
It is only because
Grief is trying its best
To stay close to the love

Forever is a long time to love someone.

*Especially when they're not here
to feel it.*

A Single Moment

There are not really words to describe that moment: the moment
you know they're gone.

It's like a clap of thunder so loud that it shouts and shrieks and shatters
the sky in two.

Like a flash of lightning so charged that it scorches and scolds and scars
the ground incessantly.

It's like an earthquake so strong that it shocks and shifts and shakes the
Earth from its axis indefinitely.

Like a storm.
A storm that starts in a single moment,
but that changes the world forever.

Except it isn't the sky,
or the ground,
or the earth.
It's you.

Your heart, your soul, your world.

That single moment shatters and shocks and shakes you...
and it leaves its mark.

And all you can do is hang on and hope that,
when the storm begins to subside,
you can learn to live with a sky, with a world, with a heart
that has been shattered in two.
Indefinitely.

Forever.

*May the salt from your tears
flow into your ocean of grief...*

And help to keep you afloat.

Somewhere To Go

Don't swallow your tears when you're grieving
'Cause the lump in your throat only grows
When you desperately try to pretend not to cry
Whilst your tears need to fall and to flow

It's like trying to pull down a mountain
So the summit's an easier reach
But you have to spend time on the difficult climb
To learn things that the mountain will teach

'Cause you can't stop the ocean from swelling
When the crashing and breaking begins
And you cannot control all the waves as they roll
But you can learn to surf them or swim

And you can't stop a storm when it's raging
It is something that can't be undone
And the weight of your pain needs the thunder and rain
To clear space in the sky for the sun

So sit with your tears when they need you
They are asking to speak and be heard
And they need a release so that they might find peace
For a while in their grief-weary world

Yes, let your tears fall when you're grieving
It will help to ease some of the load
'Cause you're likely to find all the thoughts in your mind
Are just searching...
for somewhere to go

Do not let grief rob you of your passion, my love.

*Do not swallow it
or let it silence and shrink you.*

*Instead, let it out.
Let it growl at you and grow you.*

And let it fuel your roar.

The Thing About The Heart

The thing about the heart you see,
is that its capacity to feel
is infinite.

We think it is full of love,
until grief crashes in through the cracks that loss has created.

And all of a sudden, the heart is now full of grief, love, perhaps some anger. Disbelief. Sadness, frustration, guilt.

Because the thing about the heart you see,
is that it simply expands to make room for it all.

The grief does not replace the love.
They learn to co-exist.

They might argue at first - maybe even fight – as if they're vying for heart space; and it might feel like the love is being buried beneath everything else. Beneath the anger and frustration and sadness.
But it's not, I promise.

Because the thing about the heart you see,
is its infinite capacity to grow, to expand, to make space.

And it will always make space...
It will always have space...
And it will always prioritise space
for love.

*Think of grief as a visitor
that will never leave…*

*So you might as well learn
how she takes her tea.*

On Hold

I know that this feels like being on hold
on a phone call you never wanted to make.

You wait. Hoping to hear a voice. Hoping someone answers.

Over and over you wonder if anyone is actually there, but all you hear is the same looping melody – a melody that those grieving know only too well – full of empty promises that someone will be with you shortly.

You wait.

A minute seems to stretch itself here into ten. A day drags by without you really noticing. You pace. You sit. You stare at the wall and let the song play in the background, imagining over and over that this is the moment that someone might pick up.

You could hang up. But what if you miss it? What if the voice returns while you're gone, speaking your name like nothing ever changed?

So you stay.
You wait.

And in that staying, the melody becomes part of life. You memorize the music, every rise and fall, every pause. You begin to hum along.

Sometimes you forget why you called.

But then you suddenly remember again,
and so you wait.

And whilst you know deep down that no-one is going to answer, the music somehow becomes comforting. Soothing.

And you realise that that's how it must be now:

A life that is accompanied by the melody of grief.

A life that is forever a little
on hold.

This next poem was a challenge to write, because I wanted to write something that showed how we don't become incomplete when we grieve; that the spaces left by loss - in a way that's difficult to explain – actually begin to help us make sense of the world around us: the new world – the new life – that we're navigating.

So the grey words (all the alternate words) are the spaces and the silences left behind by grief. They make sense on their own, and they are needed to make the whole thing make sense; echoing the idea that the meaning to be found in grief and loss becomes part of who we are – as a whole – even when we feel as if we're a shell of who we were before.

We are whole.
Even in grief.

Holding Space

Even in silence, grief holds deep meaning.
Even in the quiet spaces now left behind by our grief, we hold a heaviness.

Because this grief,
it gathers all the broken pieces: pieces of all our thoughts, memories and hopes and fears and...
And then it gently folds them and then weaves them together neatly, until, noiselessly, they have become all the daily breaths that we instinctively take.

So memories still linger softly in the rooms that we once thought were empty. And laughter still lives quietly in the shadows that we once assumed were silent.

Because remember this: trees will grow quietly, softly,
and clouds will gather wordlessly, without a sound;
and the morning sun? She rises even without a fanfare.

And so all these silent spaces will encourage deep growth.
So they'll gently gather all your painful pieces back together again
and quietly prove to you; you can still rise once again.

Through spaces that aren't so empty, and
silence that isn't so hollow...

My love, you will still rise,
yes
and you...

you'll finally feel,
maybe not completely whole
no,

but far less hollow, empty, heavy
than once before.

And sometimes it helps me to think that we traded places:

Part of me went with you
and part of you stayed with me.

The Ghost of Love

You'll walk past someone who's grieving today; someone who is carrying the ghost of love.

And the ghost of love is heavy: it makes the easy things difficult, and the difficult things unbearable. It weighs on every breath, every step and every turn that we take. It can make the every-day exhausting.

For some people, the ghost is a new acquaintance, and they carry it on their shoulders.
Unknown and unfamiliar, it is finding its place. Figuring out how to settle here forever.

For some it is an old friend, and they carry it in their arms.
It's almost pleasant and overly-familiar, but it can still grow heavy; and that's when it starts to ache.

And for some, it has become a part of who they are.
It walks beside them; love hand-in-hand with grief.

You'll walk past someone who's grieving today; someone weighed down by an invisible heaviness that they carry.

It's new and it's old,
and then it's old that becomes new all over again in a heartbeat.

Because, no matter how long they have known it,
that is *truly* where they carry it.

Not on their shoulders.
Not in their arms.

But always,
always
in their heart.

If loving you could bring you back...

then it wouldn't have let you go in the first place.

Rocks

I see that huge boulder of grief that you're carrying on your shoulders. Solid, unwavering. Like a mountain that you're hauling down a never-ending road.

But one day it will begin to break down into slightly smaller pieces, and you'll find that you can pack these rocks of grief into a rucksack and carry it on your back.

One day you will find a wagon, and you will load it up with those rocks, and push forward; a little more easily than before.

And one day, much further down the road, you will find that you carry your grief as pebbles in every pocket of every garment that you ever wear and will ever own.

Right now, it is this overwhelmingly huge, heavy, oppressive boulder that is threatening to flatten you at any moment.

And one day it will be that very same rock; that very same boulder. But it will be broken up differently. Scattered in pieces amongst every pocket of your whole being.

Just the same heaviness. But easier to hold.

Because that's the thing about grief:
It doesn't get lighter.

We just learn how to carry it.

If grief is an ocean,

then it is as if someone has pulled the plug and let it drain.

For how can something so vast and so deep
feel so empty?

Guide

Grief is a teacher
And loss is a lesson
But they don't have answers
To all of my questions

So many 'why?'s and 'what ifs?'
And 'what now?'
And 'when will I start to feel better?'
And 'how?'

So many questions
That fill up my thoughts
Waiting for lessons
I hope to be taught

But maybe this teacher
Is more of a guide;
A mentor, a tutor
Someone by my side

A coach, a director,
Someone on my team
Who suggests where to look
And not what should be seen

Someone who makes sure
I'm never alone
But it's up to me then
To search the unknown

And maybe it's only
By holding grief's hand
That I'll come to learn
What I must understand:

That there are no answers
No wrong and no right
Some days will be dark
And some days there'll be light

There isn't a 'how'
That will work for us all
At times we will stand
And at others we'll fall

We cannot say 'when'
Because nobody knows
How bumpy the road is
Or how far it goes

So maybe I'll pause
All the noise in my head
And sit for a while
In the quiet instead

And maybe I'll realise
Grief's not here to teach me
But rather to give you
A way you can reach me

To show me that there's
Not a right way to be
When life as you know it
Is swallowed by grief

And maybe I'll learn
There are waves I must ride
And that I have to do it
With grief as my guide

My heart is a jigsaw

and now it's missing a piece.

Shapeshifting

Grief does not shrink with time.
It doesn't dim or dull and it doesn't set itself down with the sun as she settles at dusk. Instead it lingers, like a shadow that stretches longer and leaner as the sun sinks in the sky.

Grief does not become silent with time. Instead it becomes a constant rhythm; always there but rarely quiet. A space where memories echo, and where the heart can break all over again in unexpected moments.
Like rolling waves that ebb and flow.
Like rolling clouds that swell and subside.
Like rolling thunder that roars and retreats.

No, grief does not lessen with time. It does not start to fade or disappear into nothingness. Instead, it becomes the backdrop to who we are and to everything we do. Like scenery at the back of the stage that is sometimes pulled forward; the weight of it felt anew in these moments, sparked by a song, a scent, a forgotten photograph. And in those moments, grief is as front and centre as it ever was.

Grief does not shrink, but it changes shape. It adapts to the life it must live in a world that doesn't want it. The sky gets a little wider and the ocean a little deeper. The stage makes space for it and the clouds roll in and out with it. The heart expands and the soul stretches; to take in the grief alongside the love that it longs for.

And steadily – like the seasons changing leaf by leaf, flower by flower – life grows around it;
so that after a while, we find ourselves living too.
Alongside this grief that has shaped itself around us.

Alongside this grief that has shifted continually until we are both a little more comfortable.

Alongside this grief that never learned to shrink.
But that has simply learned
to 'fit'.

Love might be a fairytale,
but grief is the tower.

Let The Grief Gather

Let your grief gather, my love.
The way you gather blankets around you when you lie in bed at night.

Let your grief weave itself into the quiet spaces between the breaths you take as you sleep, and let it settle into the corners of your heart. Let it sit with you; because grief is a patient visitor that insists on being felt and seen.
That insists on being known.

Let your grief gather,
the way the old things in the hidden spaces of your home gather dust.

Let your grief gather in the shadows, in the places where the light no longer reaches. Let it unfold like an old letter, full of memories needing to be read, acknowledged.
Needing to be known.

Let the grief you feel gather like storm clouds in a sky that thunders without asking permission. Let it gather and grow and rage.
Let it be known.

Because only when we know something, can we work with it.
Help it. Calm it.
Only when we see something for what it truly is, can we embrace it fully.
Only then can we find peace with it.

So let your grief gather,
like guests at a dinner party you never wanted to host.
Let them talk. Let them ask questions - even though you don't have the answers – and let them share their memories.
Let them rage if they need to; and let them be seen.
Let them be known.

And when they go home, after the storm dies down and the night ends; when the light once again reaches the dusty corners that were once in shadow...

Your gathered grief may just find its peace.

It's like I'm screaming into a cave,
"Come back!"

And all I can hear is my own voice repeating the same thing over and over again.

Echoes

A steady stream of echoes
Lines the path ahead of me
Each echo like a shadow
But a shadow that can speak

And all these spoken shadows
Carry heavy weights unseen
Each one a ghostly burden
That is wrapped in what has been

They whisper of the memories
And moments I hold dear
These little murmured messages
That only I can hear

They linger and resurface
Never learning to depart
Repeating and reverberating
Loudly in my heart

It's like familiar music
That keeps looping in my brain
A chorus that just keeps on playing
Time and time again

At times it's overwhelming
All this rich, resounding noise
But I don't mind because I find
It's how I hear your voice

For there are hidden harmonies
That echoed grief can bring
And that's why I choose to listen
When the speaking shadows sing

My heart is broken.
And yet it beats.

And if that is not strength in motion,
then I do not know what is.

This Too Shall Not Pass

This too shall not pass.

It is too strong, too powerful, too heavy,
and it leaves a scar.

And scars do not disappear; they do not pass.
They are a forever-reminder of what we have endured in life.

But they do fade.
They do become less painful.
They do become so much a part of us
that we grow accustomed to their presence.

And as with everything we grow accustomed to,
sometimes we don't notice it's there.

But it is, of course.

As is love.

We never think of love as a scar, and yet it is.
It is a forever-reminder of those who have enriched our life.

And if we carry one, we must carry the other:
The enrichment of love and the endurance of loss.

The beauty of love though,
is that it tends not to fade. Only grow.

So whilst both scars persist,
and whilst grief may scar a little more sharply at first...
love will win out.

It always does.

Because love too
shall not –
no, not ever –
pass.

*Someone handed me a compass
and told me it would point to you.*

It just keeps pointing towards my heart.

Taking Turns

I take my tea with milk
And with a little sugar too
I take my steak cooked medium
Not too well-done or blue

I take my morning coffee
In my very favourite cup
I take a breath and savour it
And let it warm me up

I take my time to notice
All the phases of the moon
I take a note of birdsong
And the way it changes tune

I take a daily walk
And watch the clouds as they roll by
Folding into shapes
Like origami in the sky

But now grief has arrived
And I do not know how to take it
It's not a cup of tea
And I do not know how to make it

I don't know how to sweeten it
Or stop it feeling cold
I do not wish to walk with it
Or watch it as it folds

I don't how to stomach it
Or listen as it sings
I don't know how to work through
All the phases that it brings

So I'll just have to trust it;
Let it take my peace for now
Hoping that it doesn't take
The whole of me somehow

And hopefully I'll listen
And I'll figure out and learn
That in this life of give and take
Grief needs to take its turn

*Life j st
doesn't make q ite
as m ch
sense as it sed to...*

*Now that U
are missing from it.*

Let Them Live

Why do we give flowers to the grieving?
Why do we leave bouquets at gravesides and memorials?

Why flowers?
What is it about them that brings comfort in the face of death?

Well...
maybe it's life.
Maybe the flowers are a reminder of life persevering at a time when we're overwhelmed by the loss of it.

Maybe the flowers are a reminder of the life they lived.
A reminder of the life we shared with them;
of the life of all the people around us.

And of the life we still have left.

And whilst this gentle whisper of life may be painful right now,
perhaps the flowers are there to quietly remind us that life can still bloom in the face of adversity; and it can still be beautiful. Colourful.

But it is fragile.

Yes, life is fragile, my love.

So when you're ready, go out and live it.
Make it beautiful. Make it colourful.

And until then,
whilst it still feels too painful to live like that,
accept the flowers. Nurture them. Love them.

And in the face of loss,
let them live.

Maybe we don't hold grief...

Maybe grief holds us.

Rock, Paper, Scissors

Rock
There's a stone in my pocket that I just can't throw away.
It arrived one day, heavy and you-shaped.
It didn't ask to be here and at first, I didn't want it.
But now I hold on to it. Because, although it's heavy, its presence in my pocket brings me comfort.
It helps me remember.

Paper
There's a letter under my pillow that I wrote when you left.
It helped a little to lighten the weight of that stone in my pocket.
Paper beats rock, they say. But it can't truly beat it, can't erase it. Paper doesn't crush stone, it only covers it, wraps it, softens it; like a bandage over something that will never fully heal.
But still I write. Hoping that it helps with the heaviness.

Scissors
There's a line through my life, separating then and now. Before and after. With and without you. As if someone took a pair of scissors to my world and sliced it in two. But one thing remains whole: my love.
Scissors beat paper, they say, but not this one - this paper won't tear. It is held tightly together by the words of love I wrote.
I fold that letter into a plane and let it fly, hoping it reaches you, wherever you are.

And then I reach again for that rock.
Because in this game, the rock always wins.

Because in this game, the rock is stronger than the rules.
But still...
I hold on,
I hope for healing.

And I remember.

It's like I'm waiting for you
at a station
where the train never stops

Time Waits For No-one

Oh, I thought I had time.

I thought I still had time to share with you
everything I hadn't had the chance to tell you yet.

I thought I still had time to live
alongside you before either of us had to leave.

I thought I still had time to worry
about the smallest things that never really made a difference anyway.

I thought I still had time to seek joy
in things that I hadn't made time for yet.

Because all along,
I thought that time was waiting.

I thought I still had time to breathe you in and figure you out; to learn what makes you tick.

But time ticked away from me.

And now I worry that I wasted it.
On needless concerns.
On swallowed words.
On lost joy.

But more worries do not help, because time is still ticking.

So now I will make the most of it.

I will speak the words I want to speak.
I will seek the joy I need to seek.
I will try to worry less, and I'll try to live more.

And through all of it,
I will remember...

That time is not waiting. It's ticking.

And I must make it count.

You know when you break a glass,
and thousands of tiny, sharp, almost-invisible pieces
are scattered all over the place?

That's what grief feels like.

One

Yesterday was difficult
Today might be so too
'Cause grief can make the easy things
Impossible to do

So set your expectations
Off to one side for a while
You only need to take a step
Not run a million miles

You only need to grab
The ladder's very lowest rung
Or sing a single note
And leave the others all unsung

You only need one footstep
At the bottom of the hill
And just one breath to calm you
When the world will not be still

But if you take a step
No matter how slow it might be
And then you take another
Then another two or three

Even if you find yourself
A little way off track
And even if you rest
Or take a couple of steps back

If you keep on going
You will find eventually
You've walked a mile that once
Was an impossibility

And soon there will be music
From the song that you have sung
And over time, perhaps you'll climb
To higher peaks and rungs

So take your time with grief
When it expects you to surrender
'Cause when it's overwhelming,
This is what you must remember:

Today might be quite difficult
Tomorrow might be too
But slowly, one thing at a time
My love, you'll make it through

*We don't talk about the gone
to garner sympathy or sorrow*

But rather to bring them back...

Just for a moment

I Still Say It

I still speak to you, you know.

I still say, "good morning," when I wake up and open the curtains.
Sometimes I say it aloud and sometimes I whisper it to myself.
But I still say it.

I still say, "hey you," when I walk past your chair or your photograph.
Sometimes I say it with tears in my eyes and sometimes I have a smile on my face.
But I still say it.

I still say, "what should we have for dinner?" when I get home in the evening or when I open the fridge to see what food we have in.
Sometimes I say it even though I know what I want to cook, and sometimes I'm hoping you'll give me some inspiration.
Either way, I still say it.

I still say, "it's our song!" when it plays on the radio.
I still say, "remember this?" when I find something I'd forgotten about.
I still say, "what do you think?" when I'm trying on an outfit.

I still say, "isn't it a lovely day?" and "guess who I saw!" and "what shall we watch?" and "goodnight"
and "I miss you."

And I still say, "I love you."
Whenever I see your photo. Whenever it's a lovely day.
Whenever I miss you.
Sometimes I say it aloud, sometimes in a whisper to myself; sometimes with tears in my eyes and sometimes with a smile on my face.

But always, either way,

I love you.

And I still say it.

Falling isn't always a bad thing.

Remember:
Sometimes we fall in love.

Tightrope

Grief is like a tightrope
That is stretched out long and thin
A road ahead so narrow
You don't know how to begin

The world below is distant
Like you're not part of it all
And the line ahead is fragile
One wrong move and you could fall

There's hardly space to breathe here
And you question every step
It's hard to trust your footing
When you're always on the edge

Each move becomes a challenge
As you falter and you shake
Balancing along a path
You didn't choose to take

For grief is like a tightrope
A thin and fragile line of loss
And it seems as if that's all you have
To cling to as you cross

But know that there's a safety net
In love that lies below
And it's holding out its arms
To say "I'm watching as you go"

And when you hold your arms out
To the side to steady you
That's when love grabs your hand and says,
"I'm here. We'll make it through."

*Maybe time seems to stand still in grief
because it's our way of trying to stay with the one who's gone.*

*Like, if we stand still long enough…
they'll come back and find us.*

Still Standing

In the beginning it's as if you're standing still.
You're not of course, it just feels like it.

Because your world has stopped abruptly; has stopped turning, stopped spinning. Your world has come crashing down.

And one of the toughest things to realise is that, for most other people, it has not. It has not stopped. It has not crashed.
It keeps spinning, keeps turning, and time keeps ticking.

It's like you're on a carousel; standing in one place as the world keeps moving all around you.
It's a ride you didn't choose to get on to,
and one from which you desperately wish to get off.

But you can't. The carousel keeps turning and the world keeps spinning and you are stuck standing still in the middle of it all.

Standing still.

Waiting and hoping that when the ride stops, everything will be just as it was before it started.

Except the ride won't ever stop. Not completely. But it *will* slow down.

It will slow down long enough that you won't feel so dizzy and disorientated; you won't feel so panicked and paralysed by the constant motion of life being lived around you.

It will slow down enough to let you step off once in a while. Never completely - you'll always have a ticket for this ride – but one day you will realise you can step into that life around you.
And when you do, you'll find a strength you didn't realise you had.

Your world will be different, but it will start turning again.
And you my love,
Instead of standing still...

You will be still standing.

"I'm scared that if I start crying, I'll never stop," you say.

Oh, but you will my love. Eventually.
Even the sky runs out of storms in the end.

But if the tears keep coming? That's ok.
I'm not scared of the rain.

Because for a long time now
I have known how to swim.

Stop Start

"When do I stop grieving?" you ask.

Oh my love, you do not.

Because grief only ends when love does.
It only dies when love dies and only fades as love disappears,
and so you will not stop grieving them for as long as you love them.

Instead, you start to smile again.
You start to take tentative steps forward.
You start to find pleasure in the things you enjoyed before your loss, and you start to find joy in things you are yet to discover.

It does not happen quickly or easily, and it does not happen without some steps back into the shadows sometimes.

But it does happen.
Gently.
Gradually.
When you are ready.

"When do I stop grieving?" you ask.

Oh my love, you do not.

But one day you will stop
and realise that,
without noticing,
you have started
to live again.

Would I want you to forget me?

Never.

And so I promise never to forget you either.

Skies Down

If I had a hook, I would pull down the moon
And I'd pick it apart at the seams
And I'd hold every piece knowing each had been joined
By the silvery thread of its beams

If I could lasso every star from the sky
I would gather them all to my hands
And I'd lay them before me like sequins connected
By bright golden glittery strands

If I had a net that could somehow contain
Every white, wispy, wonderful cloud
I would catch them and bring them to rest at my feet
Like a soft cotton quilt on the ground

If there was a way I could gather the sun
From its core to the end of its rays
I'd harness its fire, its warmth and its light
So that I would have sunshine each day

'Cause if there was a way I could bring down the skies
I would do it with barely a thought
Hoping that I would be closer to you
Hoping you would be something I caught

Hoping you'd land in my net, in my hands,
Hoping I could hold on to each thread
And that, just one more time, I could wrap you around me
And sit by the fire instead

But sadly I know that I can't catch the clouds
Cannot lasso the sun or the stars
And I can't pull the moon any closer towards me
Or stop you from being so far

But what I can do is keep searching the skies
'Cause I'll find you, I know, if I look
So instead of keep trying to pull the sky down
I'll remember to keep my eyes up

*There are two things that happened in my life
that proved my humanness:*

*I loved you.
Then I lost you.*

Enough

Did I tell you enough how I loved you?
Did I tell you enough to be sure?
Did I tell you enough how the jokes that you told
Made me love you a little bit more?

Did I tell you enough that I missed you
In the moments that we spent apart?
Did I tell you enough how your laugh is imprinted
Right into the walls of my heart?

Did I tell you enough or remind you
That you never stopped making me proud?
'Cause I know that I said it enough in my head
But I might not have said it aloud

Did I tell you enough you brought sunshine
Every time that you entered a place?
That you brightened the air, with the smile you would wear
That would light up the whole of your face

But now why am I asking these questions?
For I know all the answers already
And asking and wondering over and over
Is draining, exhausting and heavy

It's tiring me, getting me nowhere
Like a circle I run on the spot
'Cause I've realised the answer to all of these questions
Will always be 'no, I did not'

For it wouldn't have mattered how often,
I had spoken aloud all my love
Because even if we'd had forever,
Forever would never

have been quite enough

Birds change their song when they're sad.

I know how they feel.

Missing a Beat

Grief is not being able to get out of bed in the morning.

It's waiting for the day to end so that you can welcome back the darkness that you've come to know so well.

It's not being able to eat; and not wanting to see anyone.

Grief is wanting to shut out the world for a while and bask in the silence.

But grief is also pausing too long at the traffic lights, or zoning out of a conversation, because thoughts of them pop into your head.

It's the habit of getting two mugs out of the cupboard to make a cup of coffee in the morning; and having to put one back.

It's taking a photo you'll never show them of a view they would have loved; and smiling as you watch the tv show you always used to watch together.

Because grief is not always the deafening silence and the overwhelming darkness. It is not always rejecting the morning and retreating from life.

Sometimes it is the hum of life happening as you live it.
The tune of the everyday playing on around you.

And sometimes there will be a note that sounds flat, or a chord that's missed; just for a beat.

The whole song continues, but that flat note – that missing beat –
is grief singing its own song. Reminding you that it is everywhere and in everything.

Yes, sometimes grief is silence.

And sometimes – especially after a while - it is life
missing a beat.

And singing just a little off-key.

For my next poem, I was inspired by the poem How Do I Love Thee? (Sonnet 43).

How do I love thee? Let me count the ways.
I love thee to the depth and breadth and height
My soul can reach, when feeling out of sight
For the ends of being and ideal grace.
I love thee to the level of every day's
Most quiet need, by sun and candle-light.
I love thee freely, as men strive for right.
I love thee purely, as they turn from praise.
I love thee with the passion put to use
In my old griefs, and with my childhood's faith.
I love thee with a love I seemed to lose
With my lost saints. I love thee with the breath,
Smiles, tears, of all my life; and, if God choose,
I shall but love thee better after death.

Elizabeth Barrett Browning 1806-1861

How Do I Grieve You?

How do I grieve you? Let me count the ways.

I grieve you to the very reaches of my soul,

In a way that feels endless and deep;

In a way that I can't fully understand.

I grieve you in the simple, everyday things,

In both sunlight and candlelight; by day and by night.

I grieve you freely.

I grieve you purely.

Because I don't know how to do it any other way.

I grieve you with the same intensity of the loved we shared,

And with a rawness that serves as a constant reminder of my loss.

I grieve you for the love I had and still have for you.

I grieve you with every breath, every smile, every tear,

every moment of my life.

Yes.

I grieve you as I loved you.

If the trees can lose their limbs and their leaves in the storm and still keep reaching for the sky...

Then so can I.

Light Leaks Through

One thing I notice when waking;
When another new day's started dawning
Is how light leaks through gaps in the curtains
As the night sky fades into the morning

One thing I find when it's grey out;
When the sky fills its pockets with rain
Is how light leaks through cracks in the clouds then
Like a promise of sunshine again

And when I settle down in the evening
Something I often see at the door
Is how light creeps through right at the bottom
In the space between doorway and floor

And I notice that there is a pattern
In the way the light lingers and leaks
For it will not surrender to darkness
It's the cracks and the gaps that it seeks

As it searches for all of the spaces;
Just a sliver where it can shine through
So I wonder if light's trying to reach me
In the gaps that you left behind you

And perhaps all the cracks that I harbour
In a heart that's now peppered with holes
Are a way that the light can begin to
Shine a little warmth into my soul

Yes, one thing I notice when waking,
In the evening and when skies are grey
Is that light is completely determined
To always, *always*, find a way

Some days this loss is the hum in the background,

and some days it's the only sound I hear.

How Long Is A Piece Of String?

If loss is a piece of string,
then it's a series of knots that you have to untie.

As time goes on, the spaces between the knots will get bigger and longer, but the string is always there in the background. Looping through your every day; winding around conversations, catching on the edges of your laughter. Some days you trip on it; some days you skip with it.

You never find the end. You'll think you've reached it in a moment of peace, and then it spools again from some hidden place in your heart. It pulls tight and you remember: this string doesn't break. It frays, maybe, and softens at the edges, but it holds. It holds everything.

Loss teaches you to walk with it; to braid it into your story. To let it tether you not only to what's gone, but to what still matters. And if you follow it gently, maybe it will lead you to the love that lingers – the thing that's left after everything else unwinds and unravels.

How long is this piece of string?
Oh, it's infinite. It goes on forever.

A bit like love.

*Sometimes I sit in a room
reading, or watching tv.*

*And slowly, the light drains from the room
with the dusk.*

*I don't realise until I leave the room and come back in, wondering
how I was ever able to see what I was reading or watching.
But that's when I understand that I've been sitting in the shadows
for a while.*

And I didn't even notice.

Precious Light

"I'll leave a light on for you."

We used to say that to each other when it was dark.

Sometimes it was because one of us felt scared or apprehensive of the darkness; sometimes it was because the darkness was an unknown and unfamiliar place.

And sometimes it was because one of us simply needed to make our way home. Home to a place where someone was waiting for us.

So when the blanket of darkness fell over my life when you left, I began searching desperately for the light.

Because I was scared and apprehensive and lost.
Because the darkness was painfully unknown and unfamiliar.

And as I searched, I began to notice the silver linings at the edge of the clouds and the golden glow of the early morning sunrises. I began to watch how the sky burned bronze as the sun shed her rays, ready for nighttime.

I found the light: all the precious light that was persisting and persevering through the darkness.

And still it persists.
Still it shines.

As if you're here somewhere, somehow, saying
"I'll leave a light on for you,
so that you can find your way home.

And so you know that I'm waiting for you."

Where there's sunshine, there's shadow.

That's how joy and grief can co-exist.

A Part

I hope people know that they can say your name.

That it's not to be whispered like a secret I've forgotten,
or spoken with apology as if it has prodded my pain.

I hope people know that it is not a word they have to avoid or dance around.

I hope they realise that I want to hear your name;
I want to hear that others think about you as much as I do.
That they remember you.

And I hope they sing out your name and dance to it.
Because I want it to be shouted, celebrated, embraced.

I want you to be a part of the conversations you left behind,
and a part of the moments and the memories that lie ahead.

I want you to be a part of the laughter and a part of the tears. A part of the ordinary days and of the extraordinary times. I want you to be a part of it all.

I want you to be a part of this life
that I now must live without you.

Yes, I hope they know that they can say your name.
Say it; shout it; sing it.

So that you're here with me somehow.
In the conversations and the laughter and the ordinary moments.

So that you're a part of it all.

Even though
we are apart.

A quiet chair can still hold the weight

of someone gone.

The Griefcase

I carried round a case of grief
Though very few had known
A case so full of aches and pains
That I had never shown

A case all stacked and packed with things
I'd firmly tucked away
Because I'd thought that was the key
To keeping grief away

Then love came quiet, patient, kind,
And sat awhile with me
And suddenly a gentle click
Set what was hidden, free

For as my griefcase opened
Sadness soon came spilling out
And with it came frustration,
And denial, anger, doubt

They burst forth with an urgency
No longer trapped, confined
And so a weight was lifted
From my case and from my mind

And as they found their freedom
I watched other things arrive
Like joy and hope that now had room
Inside my case to thrive

And now within my griefcase
There's a bit of everything
Like days between the seasons
Where the winter meets the spring

There's dark and light and warmth and cold
And joy and sadness too
But that's because the grief made room
For all my love for you

I searched for you in the silence…

And you were there.
You were everywhere.

Searching

We say that we lose people; but I don't think that's strictly true.
To lose something seems to imply that it's lost. Misplaced.
And we don't misplace the ones we love.

We don't put them down and forget where we left them, only to realise they've been thrown on the counter absent-mindedly, like our keys or our wallet.

We don't count to ten and then fail to find their hiding place, only to give up when we've checked behind the trees and under the tables, like we're playing a game of hide and seek.

We don't stash them in our jeans or our jackets, only to find them a year later, tucked away like loose change in the pocket of a winter coat.

No.
We don't misplace them, but we do search.

We search for signs and synchronicities and for sunshine on rainy days.

We keep a look out for reminders of the remarkable, for the rainbows and the robins.

We search for anything that tells us they are still here in some way.

So, I don't think we lose those we love.
I think we hold onto them.
We search for them. And we find them.

We find them with us in so many ways, because loved things are never truly lost. Love is not something we misplace or hide or forget.

It is here. Always.

And if we keep looking out for it,
I think we'll find it
everywhere.

Grief walked in one day,
rearranged all the furniture,
and then sat down in your chair

Be Gentle

When I learn how you have lost someone you loved,
I will tell you to be gentle with yourself.
I will remind you to be kind to yourself, and
I will tell you to take care of yourself.

Because the truth is
that grief will not.
It will not be kind or caring or gentle.

Instead it will be harsh.
It will tear you apart, rip your heart into pieces and shatter your soul.

So I know it might sound trite.
It might sound like empty words and hollow concern,
but I promise that it isn't.

It is the way you learn, not to fight with grief, but to meet it with compassion. It is the way you learn how to respect it, honour it even.

And it's the way you get through each day: by reminding yourself that it's ok to fall apart in grief's arms.

But it's the gentleness that softens your landing as you fall. It's the gentleness that holds you whilst you shatter.

It's the kindness that picks up the pieces and remembers how they fit together; like pieces of a broken vase, reassembled so that it can still hold flowers.

So they are not empty words. They are a reminder:

Be gentle with yourself.
Be kind to yourself.

And take care of yourself.

Some days you are easy to carry.

And some days I have to lie down.

Grief is Not a Shoe Size

Grief is not a shoe size.

It is not a pair of boots that we pick off a shelf, just like many others have done before us. It is not something we can slip our feet into and think, "yes, this will fit."

Grief is a billion different shoes walking down a million different roads; in a thousand different directions, at a hundred different speeds and in many differing states of comfort.

It is not a journey we know how to take, even if we've taken it before.
It is not something we wear like others might wear theirs.

Because grief is not a shoe size.

It is not the same boots from the same shelf in the same shop.
It is not the same road, or the same direction; the same speed or the same comfort level for anyone.

It is not one-size-fits-all.
It is unique.

Love is unique from person to person; relationship to relationship.
So, it follows that our grief is too.

It is not a shoe size.
It's not supposed to 'fit', and it is not something we're supposed to slip into easily.

It is supposed to be hard and uncomfortable.
Uniquely so.

So don't be concerned with how other people are wearing their shoes. Just because they're walking a certain way, it doesn't mean you have to do the same; even if they think their way is the 'right way'.

You're not in their shoes remember.

And they're not in yours either.

I smiled today.

You would have loved that.

Everyone's Grief

Some people's grief is a wailing and weeping,
Some people's grief is a whisper
For some it's the loudest, "I'll never forget him"
For some it's a quiet, "I'll miss her"

Some will keep vigil at gravesides of loved ones
Others will cry in their sleep
For some people, grief is a noisy companion
For some, it's a secret they keep

Some people bear it by sharing with others
Some people bear it alone
But always, no matter how anyone holds it,
Everyone's grief is their own

For some it takes months to begin moving forward
For some it takes years 'til they're ready
But always remember - with each, every step -
That a journey with grief will be heavy

No-one's grief looks just like somebody else's
No two exactly alike
So do what you must to make sense of your feelings
And do what you can to get by

'Cause grief is "I miss you, I'll never forget you,"
It's vigils and talking with friends
It's whispering sometimes and other times screaming
That something has come to an end

So, bear it and hold it however you can
Whether crying in crowds or alone
And always remember, it's all of it valid
Yes, everyone's grief is their own

I hope there is a garden wherever you are.
And I hope it is blooming.

The Right Words

I was never a big fan of words – of poetry – before you.

But then I loved you, and I searched and searched for just the right words that could somehow express the strength of the love I felt.

I read that love is as deep as an ocean and as vast as the sky. That it is as infinite as the universe itself.

I read that love is the sun and the moon. Strong enough to both warm the world and turn the tides. I read that it is the meeting of souls and the connecting of hearts.

I read that, despite all the words that tried to describe it, it is indescribable.

And then I grieved you.
So now I search and search for just the right words that can somehow express the gravity of the grief I feel. And the more I read, the more I realise that the words for love are the reason that I need the words for grief.

For what is the world without warmth?
What is the sky without the sun and the moon?
What is the ocean without its tides and its depths?

They are empty. Nothing.

And that's how I feel without you.

There are not really the words to describe grief. It is indescribable.

But, if I had to try,
I would say that it is as deep as an ocean and as vast as the sky. That it is as infinite as the universe itself.

And I guess that makes sense; and it also brings me a little bit of comfort.

Because it reminds me that the reason for the gravity of my grief, is – and always will be - the strength of my love.

Grief can feel like the coldest winter,
the darkest night,
the longest storm.

But the storm will help the flowers grow.
The stars will shed some light.

And before you know it…

It will be spring.

Take My Sadness

Sometimes we need to share our sadness.

And yet, we so often apologise for it, as if our grief and our tears are an inconvenience to others. As if there is some expectation that they 'fix' things.

But grief cannot be 'fixed'; and it doesn't need to be. It needs to be acknowledged and allowed to exist without apology.

So, when I share my sadness with you,
I am not asking you to take it away.

I'm just asking you to listen,
to acknowledge.

I'm asking you to hold that sadness for a moment, whilst I give my heart a reprieve from the heaviness. The way you might take my coat from me and hang it up to rest somewhere when I come to visit.

I'm asking you to take my sadness from me and hang it someplace else for a while.

It won't be for long, and it will be there the whole time.
Sitting on the coat stand in the background, waiting to cover me again when it's time to leave.

I won't apologise for it, but I might warn you that it's heavy.

And just as I do when you take my coat,
I'll say thank you.

And I'll make sure
that whenever you need me to take your sadness, I'm ready.
Ready to take your heaviness and hang it on my coat stand in the background.

Ready to give your heart a rest.

Ready to share your sadness...
even if it's just for a while.

I've said so many difficult things in my life.

But the hardest is,
without doubt,

goodbye.

Write To Me

Write to me when I'm gone.
Write every day if you wish.

Tell me how you've filled your day,
even if it has been full of sadness and sorrow and very little else.

Turn it into words. Into poetry.

Tell me how you've spent the day shedding tears that could water an entire garden. Tell me how you long for the light to help that garden grow, but right now you feel shrouded in darkness.

Tell me that the darkness feels like a heavy blanket that somehow brings comfort, even as it weighs you down; and tell me that you both long for a moment when the weight can be lifted, but you are also scared of how vulnerable you might feel when that moment comes.

Tell me that sadness and sorrow are your friends right now. That they sit with you daily, reminding you that they do not wish to hurt you, even though it might seem that way sometimes. Tell me that you have pulled up a chair for them next to your own, and that you often fall asleep in your chair, surrounded by these friends, and under the weight of your blanket.

Write to me and tell me.

And when you wake in the morning,
and you feel the warmth of the sun through the window,
you will notice the light that you've longed for.
Sadness and sorrow will be in the next room – quieter, a little further away than before – and your blanket will be set down next to you.
You will notice the light; and you will feel it.

Write to me when I'm gone, my love.

I have my ways of writing back.

*The tears on my pillow
make the pattern of you.*

Nowhere To Go

I've often heard it said that grief is love with nowhere to go.
As if all that love is trapped inside our hearts.

So instead, I find myself thinking about where grief goes.

I think about all those tears we cry, and I realise it's grief that stains our pillows.

I think about all those flowers we lay beside headstones, and I realise it's grief that decorates our memorials.

I think about all those songs we hear that remind us of the person who's gone, and I realise it's grief that makes that music meaningful.

I think about all those people we reach out to, and I realise it is grief that encourage people to show up with compassion and kindness.

But if grief is love...

Well then it is love that stains our pillows and love that decorates our memories. It is love that reaches out and reaches in, and it is love that brings meaning and compassion to our lives.

I don't think that grief is love with nowhere to go.
I think it is love that's tied itself up in knots,
not knowing which way to turn.

It is love that has been dressed up differently.
Love in disguise; love behind a mask.

But it can go to all the same places that grief goes.

It can go to music and memories.
To prayers and to pillows.
To kindness and compassion.

And, though it might not be trapped there as we once assumed it was...
It can go – and it can stay – firmly in our hearts.

The storm came again last night.

But it's ok.
Because you are my lighthouse.

Less

Everything is less now
Like a sky of muted blue
Like something that was started
But was halted halfway through

It's like I've thrown a boomerang
That never will return
As if the sun still shines
But has forgotten how to burn

It's like I wrote a letter
That I'll never get to send
Or a riddle with no middle
That no-one can comprehend

It's like I'm on a train
And there's no way I can alight
'Cause I'm stuck inside the darkness;
There's a tunnel but no light

It's just as if I'm dreaming
Then I'm jolted wide awake
As if it's rained for days now
But the storm won't seem to break

But maybe it's because
I feel helpless against the storm
And hopeless under dull skies
Where the sun is never warm

Perhaps if I feel less
Well then, the world feels as I do:
If I'm a muted version of myself,
The world is too

So maybe if I live for 'more',
The sun will burn again
I'll finally send that letter
And I'll learn to drive that train

I'll go and chase that boomerang
And bring it to my feet
I'll choose to write the middle
So that riddle is complete

And maybe I'll hold tight
To all my dreams when I am woken
I'll put up my umbrella
'Til the storm has finally broken

I'll take back what I'm missing
Though I'll still be missing you
But I'll feel the sun again beneath
The sky's bright, bluest blue

Maybe it's not that you have to leave…

*But that those who went before you,
just couldn't wait another moment
to hold you close again.*

Stubborn Love

The hardest part of all of this
is that you are gone.
But the love is not.

The love lingers.

And even when the tears pour and the heart cries, the love doesn't leave or lessen. If anything, in these moments, it is felt more fully.

It is as if, in these moments, love doubles down, telling us in no uncertain terms that it is here to stay.
Forever.

Yes, that's what makes this so hard.

You are gone, forever.
And I will love you forever.

But though that makes it difficult to bear sometimes,
I take comfort in that too.

In how stubborn love is,
that even when it might feel as if there is no reason to stay…

It stamps its feet and stands its ground.

And refuses to be moved.

I found you.
You found me.
We found love.

Love found us.
Death found you.
Grief found me.

Love Language

Love said to Loss, "but how can you do this?
How can you leave me alone?
How can you take me so suddenly, swiftly
Away from the place I call home?"

Loss said, "oh Love, I was not trying to hurt you
I'm sorry I took them away,
I'm sorry you're lost and don't know where to go now
I wish I could show you the way."

Love said, "I don't want your empty apologies
You stole straight out of my heart.
You had to have known you were stealing what's mine
And you still went and ripped it apart."

But Loss said, "I don't know what else I should do,
Only know that I mean when I say:
I will not abandon you, leave you or lose you
I promise you Love, that I'll stay."

Then Loss held a palm out to Love, and she took it;
Together they walked hand-in-hand
And slowly but surely, they started to speak
Words that both of them could understand

And no-one else heard, understood or made sense
Of the words Love and Loss had exchanged
For their language was one that was quiet and soft
That connected them both as they changed

And that's where it started; a story of Love
And of Loss finding solace and hope
Where each found a bridge that lead back to the other
Whenever they struggled to cope

And even today, Love is walking with Loss
Sometimes dancing as well, cheek-to-cheek
Because they know that grief is the way they're connected, yes...

Grief is the language they speak

*I think I know now
how a house must feel after a hurricane,
when it's been ripped from its foundations.*

On The Fence

Grief feels like sitting on a fence between two worlds:
Before and Beyond.

The Before is a world that seems to have stopped; a life of what was, of what I had and what I held dear. A world I know so well that it pains me to remember.

The Beyond is a world that continues without pause; a life of what will be, of what is gone and what I've lost. A world I don't have a map for.

And I'm not sure how to live in Before when time has stopped there, but I don't know how to live in Beyond where time moves on regardless either.

So I sit here on the fence. One foot dangling in memory, the other in the unknown.

Getting down on the side of Before means living in the past.
Stepping down into Beyond means living without you.
And neither seems manageable right now, so I stay where I am.

It won't be forever.
But in this moment, I sit on the fence. And I find peace.

Because I find that – for now at least –
Before and Beyond stop fighting for me; stop pulling me one way or the other.
And I'm able
to simply
Be.

*And now I'm like a moth, flying round and round,
searching for a flame*

that just went out.

Grief Is A Thief

Grief may be a thief
But there are things it cannot take
Things that won't be stolen
Things it simply cannot break

It cannot steal the morning light
That each dawn ushers in
The sky still blushes into life
As each new day begins

It cannot hush a memory
Or dim the laughs we shared
Your voice still whispers, echoed
By the wind upon the air

It can't uproot the trees that stand
Unwavering and tall
Where branches still reach for the sky
And leaves still grow and fall

It cannot claim the dreams we dreamed
Or stories that we told
For still they live within us:
Ours and only ours to hold

It cannot close the open door
Or bolt the unlocked gate
Where light is sitting patiently
And hope still gently waits

For grief can't steal everything
Although it tries its best
'Cause just as seasons change
And as the rising sun will set,

And just as I keep dreaming,
And as leaves fall from the trees
This grief can't steal the parts of you
That live right here with me

When I think of you gone, I'm sad.

But I hope you know that,
when I think of your life, I'm happy.

A Candle

I feel a little like a candle these days.

Because when someone wants to talk about you;
when they say your name,
when they share a memory,
when they say "she would love this"
or "he always loved that",

it's as if they have struck a match and held it against me.

And I light up,
I ignite,
I am warmed,
knowing that your flame is being kept ablaze

by those who remember you
who speak your name,
who share your stories,
who know what you would have loved
if you were here.

And, because of that,
you *are* here.

Your flame still burns.

And so,
so does mine.

When people say, "her face lit up...", I think I know what they mean now.

Because I think that speaking of the people we love
and the memories we have with them, has the power to light us up.
To make us glow. To warm us in a way that other people notice.

So yes,
I am a little like a candle these days.

And it is always the expressions of love – always love –
that continue
to light me up.

I kept leaning into the dark
until I realised that you were most likely in the light.

So now I keep chasing the sun.

Back To Life

I'm in between right now.

I feel like I don't quite belong anywhere: I'm still alive but I'm not really living.

I'm going through the motions. I get up, I get dressed. I get breakfast, I get to work. I get through the day.

I get home,
I get dinner,
I get showered,
and I get into bed.

And the whole day feels like a dream; a bubble I'm in that never seems to pop. So close to the life around me and yet still so far away.

Everything is muted; in colour and in sound.

I know the bubble will pop one day,
even if it's just for a moment.

I know that one day I will reach out my hand and someone will take it. They won't know just how significant it is when they do, but slowly a little bit of colour will start to seep back into my life. Gradually, a little bit more noise will be bearable.

And one day, I'll get up.
I'll get dressed and I'll get breakfast.
I'll get to work, I'll get home, and I'll get dinner.

I'll get into bed.

And as I do, I'll realise that – for the first time since you left – I'd been singing in the shower.

I'll realise that I will probably always be a little in between.

But in that moment, I will breathe a little more easily.
Because I'll know that I'm slowly coming back
to life.

Music is so powerful.

*I listen to your favourite song,
and I can still hear you sing it.*

The Guilt I Felt

I remember when I first stopped crying after you'd gone…

Oh, the guilt I felt.
Did this mean I was no longer sad?

I remember the first time I smiled after you left…

Oh, the guilt I felt.
How could I smile at such a miserable time?

I remember the first time I laughed after I lost you…

Oh, the guilt I felt.
How could I indulge myself in this moment of joy when I should be feeling bereft?

But there have been times since then that I've laughed until I cried. Times when I've smiled through tears: tears of sadness, tears of joy, tears of pride.

Because I've stopped feeling guilty for finding joy amongst the sadness.

Because I've realised that a life without joy is not really a life at all. And I can't honour your life if I stop living mine.

The sadness is always there. Like the air around me, I breathe this loss day in, day out.

And for a while, that was all I could do.
Breathe.
Survive.

But now I live. I find the joy.

It's not quite the joy that I used to know. But, like an old friend, it's a joy I recognise. She looks a little different now, but she is still here.

And I'm not ready to lose her too.

Whenever I see my favourite colour…

I hope it's you that put it there.

When You Visit

My darling, when you visit me
Please promise me you'll leave
A little gift each time you're here
To help me as I grieve

Please scatter little feathers
Bright as winter's whitest snow
Beside the blue forget-me-nots
As they begin to grow

Please teach that friendly cardinal
The songs you loved to sing
And keep a group of snowdrops
Blooming all the way through spring

Leave me lots of pennies
That I'll pick up from the ground
And still the stormy, wilful wind
Each time you come around

Because the coins and cardinals
Will help me know you're near
They'll be the hug that holds me
When your arms cannot be here

So darling, when you visit me
Please leave a little sign
Bring presents in your presence
That you plan to leave behind

So when I find a penny
In your favourite walking spot
And see white snowdrops growing
Next to blue forget-me-nots

And when I smell your scent
Or see a rainbow up above
I'll know you've come to visit
And to wrap me in your love

I've tucked you into my pocket
so I can take you
wherever I go

Daffodils

In grief my love,
look for the daffodils.

It may not be actual daffodils of course.
It might in fact be the sunrise outside your window as you draw back the curtains one morning.
It might be the decision to draw back the curtains at all, after weeks of being comforted by the dark.

It might be walking past their photo and smiling instead of crying; or picking up that empty mug on the coffee table that hasn't been moved since they left.

It might be a message from a friend that you now feel ready to answer; and it might be that meal you cook for yourself after days of surviving on not very much at all.

Because in the winter of grief,
these are all signs of spring; they are the beacons of hope that perhaps there are lighter days to come. Days that are a little less harsh. Less dark. Less bleak.

Winter always comes back of course, and so there will be times when the darkness returns: when you find solace in the closed curtains and in the empty mugs.

But each time,
remember to hold on to hope. To the signs of spring.

Remember to look for the daffodils.

I hear people say, "good grief,"
and I wonder if there can really be anything good about grief.

And then I remember..
of course there can.

The love.

Pitter Patter

It can feel like a storm at first, loss.

Like heavy rain, flooding your world, leaving so many puddles that you simply can't avoid them. Puddles so deep that you feel you could drown in them.

And the truth is that the rain never leaves.
It only changes, into something more like raindrops on a roof.

A steady drip
      drop
      drip
      drop
that murmurs in the background.

A steady tick
      tock
      tick
      tock
that reminds you that the world keeps turning.

It isn't loud and it isn't heavy; but it's constant.

And there is something comforting about its presence, its persistence. Something reassuring about its rhythm and its resonance.

It doesn't leave deep puddles so freely
and it doesn't threaten to flood you so often.

It simply pitter-patters in the background, like a tap
                                      tap
                                      tap on the window
                                      reminding you it's here.

Like a recurring dream with a steady beat, or footsteps on a well-known path. Like an echo from the storm, whispering softly and constantly I
                                                          love
                                                          you.

*Just think of the day
when you run into my open arms
again.*

I Hope You Find Hope

And in the end,
I hope you find hope.

Because I think that hope is the antidote to this darkness you feel. Not in the sense that it takes it away; but in the sense that it brings a flicker of light to the shadows.

Hope does not remove or reverse what has gone before, but I think it can pave a slightly easier path to the future. Maybe not initially, but ultimately.

It is a path that will likely lead to somewhere new, or to somewhere familiar but changed. Somewhere that doesn't feel or look quite as you have been used to, but hopefully it's a place of some peace.

Because the storms come.
But they also pass eventually. And even when we think we can't...

We make it through,
the sun peeks around the clouds
and those silver linings remind us that,
no matter how dark and stormy the sky gets, the sun is still there.

Shining.
Beaming.

Waiting to lend us some light.

No matter what you've been told, my love…
you do not need to let go of grief.

Hug it. Hold it.
Cling to it if you must.

It will remind you of how fiercely you love.

Signs

There's a robin on my fence today,
A feather by my feet
A heart-shaped leaf that blows along
Beside me down the street

Your song played on the radio
This morning in the car
And just last night I could've sworn
I saw a shooting star

The sun and rain are dancing
Making rainbows in the sky
And on the slightest breeze I watch
A butterfly go by

And people might say these are not
The signs I know they are
That it is just coincidence
Your song played in the car

That it is just the sky
And it is just the birds and breeze
A little windy weather
And the nature of the trees

But there is nothing little
About the way they make me feel
The sense of peace they carry
Is both comforting and real

Because it's just one song
And just one butterfly and bird
Just one star and just one leaf
In one enormous world

And so the probability
Of noticing it all
Is close to nearly nothing
Almost infinitely small

And that is how I know
That when that leaf floats into view
It isn't a coincidence,
But a sign of love from you

So keep on shooting stars to me,
Keep playing me your song
Whilst you dance atop the rainbows
And blow heart-shaped leaves along

Yes, keep on sending signs my love
I'll always look around
For your butterflies on breezes
And your feathers on the ground

*They say that we're at rest
when we die.*

*But I really hope
I'm dancing.*

ABOUT THE AUTHOR

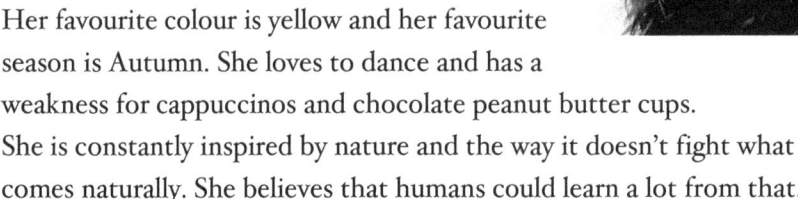

This book is Becky's sixth collection. She has published four general poetry collections (two rhyming and two non-rhyming), and with this book, she now has two collections of grief and loss poetry.

Her favourite colour is yellow and her favourite season is Autumn. She loves to dance and has a weakness for cappuccinos and chocolate peanut butter cups. She is constantly inspired by nature and the way it doesn't fight what comes naturally. She believes that humans could learn a lot from that.

When she's not writing poetry, she is walking amongst the trees, marvelling at the moon and reading light and fluffy romance novels (because some things in life might not always have a happy ending but it does no harm to spend time in stories that do).

She can be found hanging out at the places below - some more frequently than others - and the easiest way to contact her (and subscribe to her newsletter) is via email at info@beckyhemsley.com.

Facebook: facebook.com/talkingtothewild
Instagram: Instagram.com/beckyhemsleypoetry
TikTok: tiktok.com/@talkingtothewild
Pinterest: pinterest.com/talkingtothewild
Etsy: etsy.com/uk/shop/talkingtothewild
X: twitter.com/hemsleybecky
YouTube: youtube.com/@beckyhemsleypoetry5560
Website: beckyhemsley.com

All links can be accessed by scanning the QR code above.

www.ingramcontent.com/pod-product-compliance
Lightning Source LLC
Chambersburg PA
CBHW041305240426
43661CB00011B/1023